The Real World of Pirates

PIRATE SHIPS

SAILING THE HIGH SEAS

By Liam O'Donnell

Consultant:
Sarah Knott, Director
Pirate Soul Museum
Key West, Florida

Capstone
press®

Mankato, Minnesota

Edge Books are published by Capstone Press,
151 Good Counsel Drive, P.O. Box 669, Mankato, Minnesota 56002.
www.capstonepress.com

Library of Congress Cataloging-in-Publication Data
O'Donnell, Liam, 1970–
    Pirate ships: sailing the high seas / by Liam O'Donnell.
    p. cm.—(Edge Books. The real world of pirates)
    Summary: "Presents different types of pirate ships and their features, how
they were obtained, their uses and care, and some of the famous pirates who used
them"—Provided by publisher.
    Includes bibliographical references and index.
    ISBN-13: 978-0-7368-6427-5 (hardcover)
    ISBN-10: 0-7368-6427-X (hardcover)
    1. Pirates—Juvenile literature. 2. Sailing ships—Juvenile literature.
I. Title. II. Series.
G535.O37 2007
910.4'5—dc22   2005035969

Editorial Credits
Aaron Sautter, editor; Thomas Emery, designer; Tom Alvarado and Tod Smith,
    illustrators; Kim Brown, production artist; Wanda Winch and Charlene Deyle,
    photo researchers

Photo Credits
The Bridgeman Art Library/Private Collection/*The Buccaneers*,
    Waugh, Frederick Judd (1861–1940), 19
Corbis/Bettmann, 16–17; Images.com/Christopher Zacharow, 11;
    Joel W. Rogers, 24–25
Cranston Fine Arts, 14–15
Image courtesy of modelshipmaster.com, Westminster, CA, 21
North Wind Picture Archives, 8–9, 13
Peter Newark's Historical Pictures, 6–7, 20
Peter Newark's Pictures, 4–5, 7, 12, 28–29
Shutterstock/T.W., 22–23
Tod Smith, 26–27

TABLE OF CONTENTS

CHAPTERS

4 Pirates and Their Ships

10 Fast and Sturdy Ships

17 How to Get a Pirate Ship

22 Types of Pirate Ships

FEATURES

26 Parts of a Pirate Ship

30 Glossary

31 Read More

31 Internet Sites

32 Index

Chapter One

PIRATES AND THEIR SHIPS

When merchant ship crews grew unhappy with their captain, they sometimes took control of the ship.

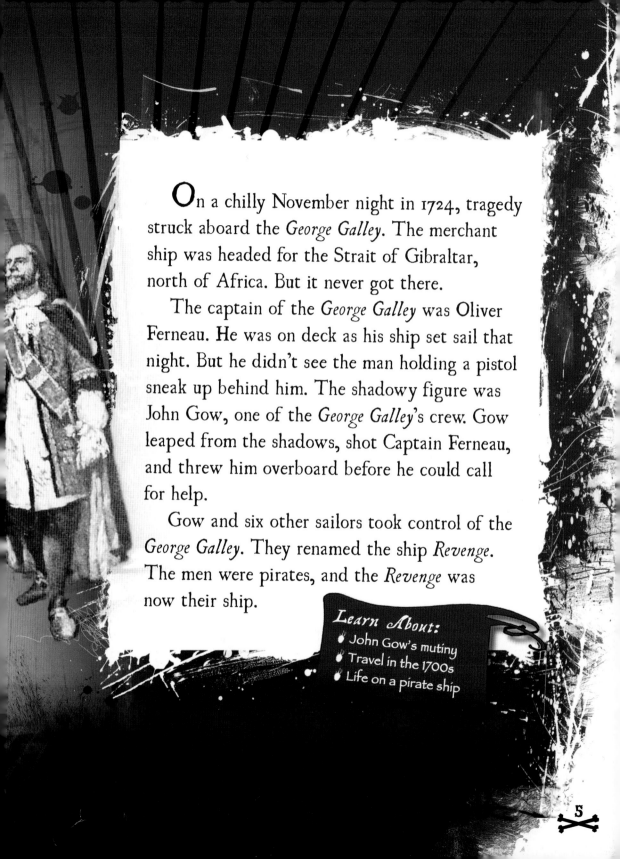

On a chilly November night in 1724, tragedy struck aboard the *George Galley*. The merchant ship was headed for the Strait of Gibraltar, north of Africa. But it never got there.

The captain of the *George Galley* was Oliver Ferneau. He was on deck as his ship set sail that night. But he didn't see the man holding a pistol sneak up behind him. The shadowy figure was John Gow, one of the *George Galley*'s crew. Gow leaped from the shadows, shot Captain Ferneau, and threw him overboard before he could call for help.

Gow and six other sailors took control of the *George Galley*. They renamed the ship *Revenge*. The men were pirates, and the *Revenge* was now their ship.

Learn About:
- John Gow's mutiny
- Travel in the 1700s
- Life on a pirate ship

Early Ship Travel

Today, airplanes and big steel ships carry people and goods across the ocean. But during the 1700s, the only way to travel across the ocean was in leaky wooden ships. Merchant ships carried people and valuable cargo like gold, rare spices, or precious jewels to countries around the world.

Merchant ships carried valuable cargo, but were usually only lightly armed. They were easy prey for pirates.

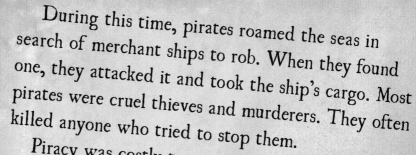

During this time, pirates roamed the seas in search of merchant ships to rob. When they found one, they attacked it and took the ship's cargo. Most pirates were cruel thieves and murderers. They often killed anyone who tried to stop them.

Piracy was costly to countries around the world. Many merchant ships were lost due to pirates, along with the gold and cargo the ships carried. Many countries sent navy ships to bring pirates to justice. Some countries even hired private ship owners, or privateers, to hunt them down.

Heavily armed navy ships were often sent to hunt down pirates.

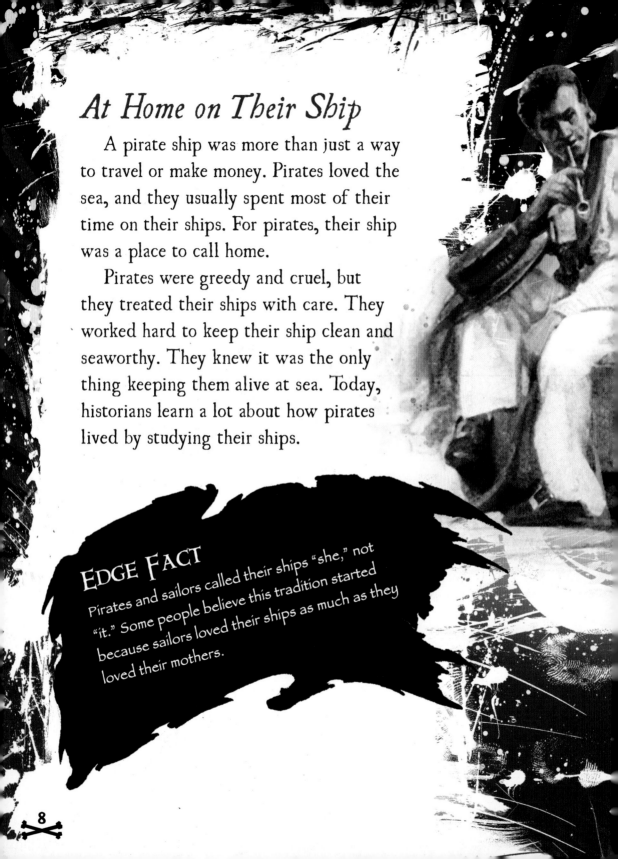

At Home on Their Ship

A pirate ship was more than just a way to travel or make money. Pirates loved the sea, and they usually spent most of their time on their ships. For pirates, their ship was a place to call home.

Pirates were greedy and cruel, but they treated their ships with care. They worked hard to keep their ship clean and seaworthy. They knew it was the only thing keeping them alive at sea. Today, historians learn a lot about how pirates lived by studying their ships.

EDGE FACT

Pirates and sailors called their ships "she," not "it." Some people believe this tradition started because sailors loved their ships as much as they loved their mothers.

When pirates were not fighting battles or caring for their ships, they took time to relax and enjoy life at sea.

Chapter Two

FAST AND STURDY SHIPS

Pirates spent much of their time hunting for merchant ships or running from pirate hunters. The most successful pirates had ships that were fast, sturdy, and well armed.

Speedy Ships

Most pirate ships were designed to sail fast. Small, narrow ships could easily cut through the water to catch merchant ships. Others were built for easy steering. These ships turned faster than bigger ships could, allowing for easy escapes from pirate hunters.

A ship's speed came from its sails. The more sails a ship had, the faster it moved across the water. Some ships had up to three masts that held as many as 20 sails.

Learn About:
- Ship design
- Repairing ships
- Ship weapons

Large ships with many sails moved swiftly across the sea.

Safe and Strong Ships

Pirates sailed long distances in search of treasure. During their many weeks at sea, pirates often sailed their ships through fierce storms. Pirate ships had to be seaworthy to withstand heavy rain and strong winds.

Shipwrecks at sea were a danger to all pirates. Strong storms and large waves could smash a ship against sharp rocks along a coast. The rocks could break the ship's hull, causing the ship to sink. Many pirates died in shipwrecks.

Pirates worked hard to keep their ships seaworthy. They fixed leaks, replaced rotting boards, and scraped small shellfish called barnacles off the ship's hull.

Ships had to be sturdy enough to survive nasty storms.

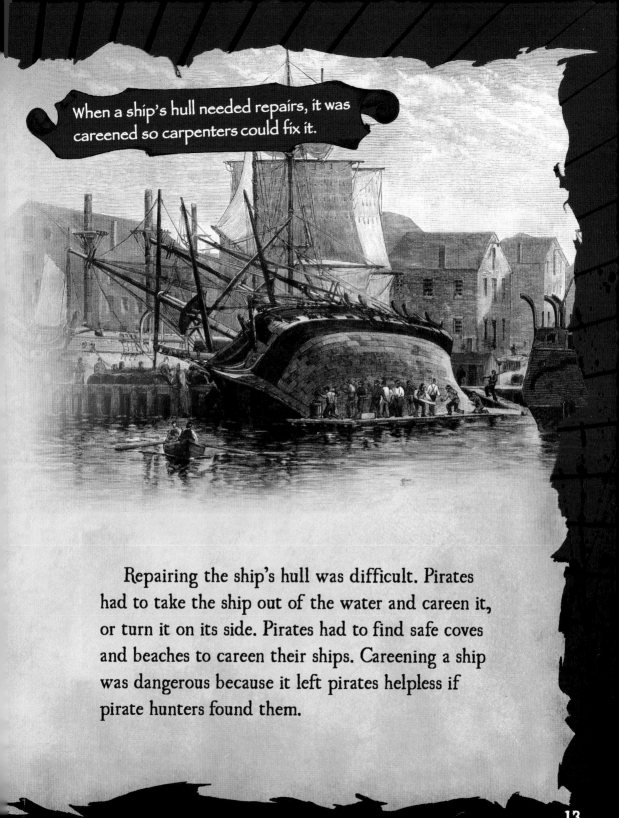

When a ship's hull needed repairs, it was careened so carpenters could fix it.

Repairing the ship's hull was difficult. Pirates had to take the ship out of the water and careen it, or turn it on its side. Pirates had to find safe coves and beaches to careen their ships. Careening a ship was dangerous because it left pirates helpless if pirate hunters found them.

Pirates didn't win every battle. In 1722, "Black Bart" Roberts lost this battle against the *Swallow*, a British naval ship.

Well-Armed Ships

Pirates fought brutal battles against merchant ships, navy ships, and pirate hunters. Well-armed ships helped pirates win many of these battles. Pirates often added extra cannons and guns to their ships. The cannons extended from the side of the ship through holes called gunports. Cannons fired different kinds of ammunition, including cannon balls and grape shot, that caused lots of damage to an enemy ship.

Edge Fact

Some merchant ships had false gunports marked on their sides. Merchant captains hoped the false gunports would fool pirates into thinking their ships were heavily armed.

Pirates often looked for bigger, better-armed ships that they could take for themselves.

Chapter Three

HOW TO GET A PIRATE SHIP

Pirates got their ships the same way they got most things—they stole them. When pirates raided a merchant ship, they often took it for themselves. Sometimes, a ship's crew would turn against their captain in a mutiny. They took control of the ship and began to use it for their pirate raids.

Revolting Crews

In the 1700s, the life of a navy sailor was hard. Some ship captains were very cruel. Beatings and other punishments were common. When sailors mutinied, it was usually violent. Often, the sailors either killed their captain or marooned him on a deserted island.

Learn About:
- Mutinies
- The Adventure Galley
- Blackbeard's ship

Mutinies happened on merchant ships too. One of the most peaceful mutinies happened in 1694 on the ship *Charles II*. The ship's captain was asleep when a sailor named Henry Every and some of the crew took control. When the captain awoke, Every told him, "I'll let you into a secret. I am the captain of this ship now." Every let the captain row a small boat back to shore. Every then renamed the ship the *Fancy* and soon became one of the most feared pirates sailing the seas.

Ships as Treasure

Sometimes the most valuable treasure from a captured ship was the ship itself. Pirates were always hunting for faster, stronger, and better-armed ships. If a pirate captain liked the ship he captured, he would add it to his fleet. The pirate captain would put a crew member in charge of the new ship, and they would sail together as a group.

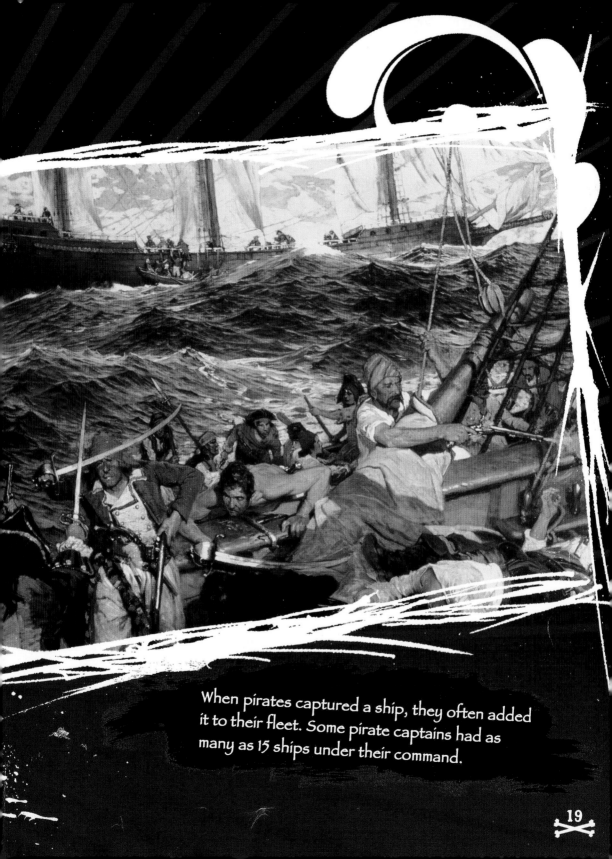

When pirates captured a ship, they often added it to their fleet. Some pirate captains had as many as 15 ships under their command.

Famous Pirate Ships

One of history's most successful pirates was Bartholomew Roberts, or Black Bart. In his career, he captured more than 400 ships, along with countless treasures. Whenever he found a ship he liked, he claimed it as his own. He gave each of them similar names such as *Fortune*, *Great Fortune*, and *Royal Fortune*.

In 1695, Captain William Kidd became a pirate hunter with his new ship, the *Adventure Galley*. But when Captain Kidd couldn't find any pirates, he decided to become one himself. Soon, Captain Kidd and the *Adventure Galley* were feared around the world.

EDGE FACT

The *Adventure Galley* was built for speed, fighting battles, and holding treasure. It had no sleeping rooms or kitchen. The ship's 150 pirates slept wherever they could find room.

Queen Anne's Revenge

Blackbeard's Fleet

One of the most famous and most feared pirates of all time was Edward Teach, also known as Blackbeard. He got his name from the huge black beard that covered his face. With his long, braided beard and a wild look in his eyes, he easily struck fear into the hearts of his victims.

Blackbeard's ship, the *Queen Anne's Revenge*, was widely feared on the seas. Armed with nearly 40 cannons and weighing 200 tons (181 metric tons), it was one of the largest pirate ships in history. The ship's large size, along with Blackbeard's reputation, scared many merchant ship captains into surrendering without a fight.

At the height of his career, Blackbeard had a fleet of four captured ships and commanded nearly 400 pirates. In 1718, many of Blackbeard's men were sick and in need of medicine. To get it, Blackbeard anchored his fleet at the harbor of Charleston, South Carolina. He began raiding ships and kidnapping citizens of the city. To end the blockade and return the captives, the governor gave Blackbeard the money and medicine he demanded.

Chapter Four
TYPES OF PIRATE SHIPS

Each pirate had a favorite type of ship. Some pirates liked sailing small, fast ships that could sneak up on merchant ships and make quick getaways. Other pirates showed their strength by sailing large ships that carried many cannons.

Schooners

Schooners were a pirate favorite. Schooners were small, narrow ships with two tall masts. They were some of the fastest ships on the sea. Most schooners carried about 75 pirates and eight cannons.

Schooners could also sail in very shallow water. Pirates often sailed schooners in narrow channels between islands where large navy ships couldn't find them.

Learn About:
- Kinds of ships
- Parts of a ship
- "Making her flush"

Pirates liked schooners because they were fast and small enough to hide from pirate hunters.

Sloops

The sloop was a perfect ship for many pirates. Sloops were small, fast, and easy to steer. A sloop had only one center mast. It also had a long pole called a bowsprit that stretched out from the front of the ship. Sails mounted along the bowsprit gave the sloop extra speed. Sloops could carry about 75 pirates and 14 cannons.

Square-Riggers

One of the biggest pirate ships was the square-rigger. It was slower than a sloop or schooner, and it was harder to steer. But pirates liked them because their large size scared many merchant ship crews. Square-riggers had up to three masts, carried 200 pirates, and could fire 20 or more cannons.

Square-riggers were named for the shape of their sails. The large, square sails helped these big ships sail long distances.

Parts of a Pirate Ship

Captain's quarters

Cannons

Rudder

Sail locker

Mainmast

Galley (kitchen)

Anchor

Cargo hold

Battles were deadly for even the fiercest pirates. Blackbeard was killed in this battle against British Lieutenant Robert Maynard in 1718.

Pirate Ship Makeovers

Pirates often changed their ships to meet their needs. They cut gunports in the sides of their ships to add extra cannons. They also knocked down walls below the deck to make more room for the crew to fire the weapons.

Sometimes pirate carpenters made the ship's deck all one level. They called this work "making her flush." A deck that was all one level made fighting battles easier. It also let the pirates easily jump onto merchant ships.

Pirate Ships Today

The days of pirates and their ships have passed, but their stories continue to thrill us. Today, treasure hunters search for lost pirate ships and the gold they once held. Historians study shipwrecks to learn how pirates once lived. Hundreds of years after they sailed the high seas, pirate ships still have much to teach us about the real world of pirates.

Glossary

barnacle (BAR-nuh-kuhl)—a small shellfish that attaches itself to the sides of ships

blockade (blok-AYD)—to close off an area to stop people or supplies from going in or out

bowsprit (BOU-sprit)—a long pole that extends from the front of a ship and holds the front sails

careen (kuh-REEN)—to turn a ship on its side to clean or repair the hull

maroon (muh-ROON)—to be left alone on a deserted island

mast (MAST)—a tall, strong pole in the center of a ship that holds the ship's main sails

mutiny (MYOOT-uh-nee)—a revolt against the captain of a ship

seaworthy (SEE-wurth-ee)—fit or safe for sea voyage

Read More

Platt, Richard. *Pirate*. DK Eyewitness Books. New York: DK Publishing, 2004.

Steer, Dugald. *Pirateology: The Pirate Hunter's Companion*. Ologies. Cambridge, Mass.: Candlewick Press, 2006.

Williams, Brian. *Pirates*. A First Look at History. Milwaukee: Gareth Stevens, 2005.

Internet Sites

FactHound offers a safe, fun way to find Internet sites related to this book. All of the sites on FactHound have been researched by our staff.

Here's how:

1. Visit *www.facthound.com*

2. Choose your grade level.

3. Type in this book ID **073686427X** for age-appropriate sites. You may also browse subjects by clicking on letters, or by clicking on pictures and words.

4. Click on the **Fetch It** button.

FactHound will fetch the best sites for you!

Index

Adventure Galley, 20

battles, 14, 15, 20, 29
Blackbeard, 21, 28
bowsprit, 24

cannons, 15, 21, 23, 24, 25,
    26, 29
captains, 15, 17, 18, 20
careening, 13
cargo, 6, 7, 27
Charles II, 18

Every, Henry, 18

Fancy. See *Charles II*
Ferneau, Oliver, 5
fleets, 18, 21

George Galley, 5
Gow, John, 5
gunports, 15, 29

Kidd, William, 20

marooning, 17
masts, 10, 23, 24, 26, 27
merchant ships, 5, 6, 7, 10, 15,
    17, 18, 21, 23, 24, 29
mutinies, 5, 17, 18

navy ships, 15, 23

pirate hunters, 7, 10, 13,
    15, 20

Queen Anne's Revenge, 21

raids, 7, 17
Revenge. See *George Galley*
Roberts, "Black Bart," 14, 20

sails, 10, 24, 26
schooners, 23, 24
ship design, 10, 23–25, 28
shipwrecks, 12, 29
sloops, 24
speed, 10, 20, 23, 24
square-riggers, 25
stealing ships, 5, 17–18
steering, 10, 24

Teach, Edward. *See* Blackbeard
treasure, 6, 12, 18, 20, 29